Stop Smoking

A Comprehensive And Accessible Manual Providing Step By Step Instructions For Effortless Smoking Cessation, Conquering Persistent Tobacco Dependency, And Achieving Long Lasting Freedom From Withdrawal Symptoms

Eugene Mullen

TABLE OF CONTENT

Organizing Your Exit Strategy: Establishing A Date To Cease And Crafting A Comprehensive Strategy 1

The Habit Of Cigarette Smoking 17

The Physiological And Psychological Hold Of Nicotine 39

The Subjugation Of Minds: Unveiling The Influence Of Advertising And Societal Conformity In The Promotion Of Smoking 72

Understanding Nicotine Addiction 101

Strategies For Ceasing The Habit Of Smoking 119

Stopping Gradually 143

Organizing Your Exit Strategy: Establishing A Date To Cease And Crafting A Comprehensive Strategy

Congratulations on taking the important Strategies for smoking cessation! Establishing a designated cessation date and formulating a comprehensive plan are vital measures in your endeavor to lead a tobacco-free existence. Below are a few suggestions to aid you in your preparation:

Designate a cessation date: Select a date in the immediate future that is convenient for you, and document it on your calendar. This will provide you with a concrete objective to strive for and facilitate your psychological readiness for the impending transformation.

Recognize your stimuli: Be mindful of the specific instances and circumstances in which smoking typically occurs. Do you engage in smoking following your meals? When you\\\'re stressed? When in the company of specific individuals? Having an awareness of your triggers enables you to devise strategies for both circumventing and effectively handling them.

Designate your network of support: Inform your relatives, acquaintances, and colleagues of your intentions to cease smoking. Kindly seek their assistance and motivational backing. Please contemplate the option of joining a support group or enlisting the assistance of certified professionals if you perceive the need for further support.

Compile a comprehensive inventory of motivations for cessation: Record an exhaustive catalogue enumerating the various rationales prompting your desire to abstain from smoking. Please ensure that you retain this list and consult it as a point of reference whenever you experience the urge to indulge in smoking.

Formulate adaptive mechanisms: Deliberate upon alternative approaches to manage stress or other emotions that may elicit your inclination to smoke. This may comprise physical activity, contemplation, diaphragmatic breathing, or alternative stress-relief methodologies.

Eliminate smoking stimuli: Dispose of all tobacco products, ignition devices, and receptacles associated with smoking in your residence, vehicle, and professional environment. This will effectively mitigate the urge to engage in smoking behavior.

Contemplate the potential of nicotine replacement therapy: Engage in conversation with your medical practitioner regarding the employment of nicotine replacement therapy (NRT), including patches, gum, or lozenges. These aids have the potential to mitigate cravings and alleviate the symptoms associated with withdrawal.

Establish achievable objectives: Divide your overarching aim to quit smoking into more manageable and realistic milestones. As an illustration, one could initiate the process by reducing the daily consumption of cigarettes, or by consciously abstaining from smoking in specific circumstances.

Grant yourself a deserving reward: Provide oneself with constructive affirmation upon the accomplishment of each objective. This can serve as a source of encouragement to persevere. Indulge in something that brings you pleasure, such as a preferred culinary delight, a film of your choosing, or a fresh addition to your wardrobe.

Engage in physical activity: Regular exercise has been proven to effectively alleviate stress and enhance emotional well-being, thereby facilitating the management of cravings and withdrawal symptoms. Make an effort to include a type of physical activity in your daily regimen, such as engaging in walks, runs, or practicing yoga.

Engage in the practice of mindfulness: Cultivating mindfulness enables one to maintain a steadfast awareness of the present moment, ensuring an ability to deflect cravings and detrimental thoughts. Engage in the cultivation of mindfulness through the utilization of techniques such as meditation or the implementation of deep breathing exercises.

Be ready to encounter withdrawal symptoms: Common manifestations of withdrawal may encompass irritability, anxiety, headaches, and sleep disturbances. Having awareness of what to anticipate can assist in making necessary preparations. Please contemplate consulting with your healthcare provider for guidance on strategies to effectively address and mitigate these symptoms, such as therapeutic intervention or pharmacological interventions.

Maintain an optimistic outlook: Ceasing the habit of smoking presents a formidable journey, albeit one that paves the way to enhanced well-being and an elevated standard of living. Maintain your focus on the advantages derived from the act of cessation, encompassing enhanced respiratory abilities, diminished susceptibility to ailments, and the potential for substantial financial savings by abstaining from the purchase of tobacco products.

Please be mindful that the process of giving up smoking is a continuous path rather than a fixed endpoint. It is imperative to exercise patience towards oneself and maintain unwavering commitment to one's objective. By adequately preparing and receiving ongoing assistance, one can effectively cease smoking and derive immense advantages from a life free from the habit's influence.

Tip 5

Inform individuals of your intention to resign.

These individuals constitute a valuable network of support, therefore, I encourage you to inform your acquaintances, relatives, and loved ones about their availability and willingness to assist you throughout this endeavor.

You may consider participating in online forums and groups dedicated to individuals who are also in the process of quitting. Within these communities, like-minded individuals can offer support, exchange valuable tips, and discuss relevant experiences. There is a wide array of forums available to join, and you can even contribute to the dialogue by leaving comments on YouTube videos, providing an opportunity for others to benefit from your insights. If you have reached this juncture in the book, you deserve commendation for your determination to quit, which is indeed excellent news. Now, let us redirect our attention to the aforementioned steps, wherein we shall proceed to discuss the various health advantages attained through the act of quitting.

The advantages of ceasing tobacco use

Numerous advantages exist, however, let us commence with the fundamental aspects.

Let us begin with the initial step: after you have smoked your last cigarette and have now quit, a mere 20 minutes later, your heart rate will commence a deceleration process, which is a positive development. Additionally, within a span of 48 hours, or at the conclusion of this timeframe, the accumulation of hazardous carbon monoxide within your bloodstream will be thoroughly eliminated. Consequently, you will experience reduced fatigue, improved respiration, enhanced sleep, heightened gustatory sensations, increased vitality, teeth of a whiter shade, fresher breath, and clearer skin. Moreover, the act of quitting smoking will substantially diminish your susceptibility to developing lung, oral, and

throat cancer.

The following aspect to consider is the enhancement of your immune system. Upon ceasing smoking, your immune system will experience a substantial improvement, resulting in accelerated healing and reduced susceptibility to illnesses. In fact, there are numerous other advantages associated with quitting smoking, which I have provided in a comprehensive list below for your reference. Lastly, one cannot disregard the financial benefits that will arise from the savings accrued by abstaining from this habit.

Please take note that I acknowledge the challenges associated with quitting, and I trust that you share the same understanding.

Given your understanding of the scientific principles underlying this matter and your ability to effectively discontinue the relevant behaviors, I extend my sincerest wishes for success in all of your endeavors. I sincerely trust that the guidance provided in this publication will prove beneficial to you. It is worth noting, however, that quitting is a challenging endeavor and there is a possibility of experiencing relapses. This occurrence is entirely normal. Nevertheless, armed with the knowledge and strategies outlined in this book, I have full confidence that you possess the capability to overcome setbacks and achieve your goal. I sincerely wish that these tips prove to be beneficial for you.

One: A Comprehensive Exploration of Substance Dependency

Gaining insight into the inclination to engage in smoking is an essential initial phase in cessation.

1. Nicotine exhibits a marked propensity for addiction: Nicotine serves as the

principal addictive compound found in tobacco products. Upon inhalation, nicotine swiftly crosses into the brain, eliciting a euphoric sensation that facilitates the development of addiction in individuals.

2. Smoking leads to the activation of dopamine production, as dopamine serves as a neurotransmitter associated with sensations of pleasure and reinforcement. Smoking induces the release of dopamine, thereby reinforcing the behavior and rendering cessation more challenging.

3. Nicotine withdrawal can present significant difficulties: Individuals attempting to abstain frequently encounter withdrawal symptoms, including heightened feelings of anger, anxiety, and difficulty concentrating. Managing these indicators can be difficult, and they have the potential to lead to a repetition of the condition.

4. Quitting can be challenging due to the presence of triggers: The act of smoking is frequently associated with specific triggers, including feelings of concern or unease, social gatherings, and certain periods of the day. Recognizing and managing these factors is a crucial component of smoking cessation.

5. Nicotine replacement therapy can be efficacious: Nicotine replacement therapy, such as the administration of nicotine gum or patches, can be effective in managing withdrawal symptoms and reducing the intensity of cravings. It is imperative to consult with a healthcare professional prior to commencing any nicotine replacement regimen.

.

Two: Prevalent Catalysts Encouraging Smoking Behavior

Concern: A significant number of individuals resort to smoking as a means of managing their anxiety. Individuals may experience a desire or strong inclination for a cigarette as a means of alleviating their heightened anxiety levels when confronted with a psychologically demanding circumstance.

Social contexts: Smoking frequently correlates with social challenges, such as gatherings or intermissions during professional engagements. Being in the presence of individuals who smoke or experiencing pressure to conform may elicit the desire to smoke.

Alcohol consumption: The consumption of alcohol may reduce inhibitions, thereby increasing the propensity for smoking. There are numerous assertions claiming that individuals tend to engage in increased tobacco consumption during alcohol consumption.

Regimen and custom: Smoking can assimilate into an individual's daily regimen, such as post-meal periods or during vehicular travels. These routines can be challenging to discontinue and could engender strong desires.

Psychological states: Individuals may engage in smoking as a coping mechanism for feelings of sadness, anxiety, or monotony.

To identify the underlying factors contributing to your smoking habit, consider maintaining a comprehensive record documenting the instances and reasons for your smoking behavior. This can assist in identifying patterns and comprehending the specific circumstances or emotional states that trigger certain impulses. Once an individual has identified their triggers, they can proceed to devise strategies to effectively manage them. This may involve seeking alternative mechanisms to deal with stress or deliberately avoiding social environments that commonly facilitate smoking. Effectively managing stressors is a vital component in achieving abstinence from smoking and maintaining a smoke-free lifestyle.

The Habit Of Cigarette Smoking

The habit of smoking poses a formidable challenge, ensnaring numerous individuals across the globe. It constitutes a complex interplay of physical dependence, psychological stimuli, and societal influences that perpetuate individuals' enslavement to a detrimental behavior accompanied by significant health repercussions. This essay delves into the intricacies of smoking addiction, examining its origins, the role of nicotine, and the numerous challenges it presents.

The Cycle of Dependence

Central to the smoking addiction rests a recurring pattern of dependence that can prove formidable to overcome. The initiation of this process commences with an individual's initial encounter with nicotine found in cigarettes. Nicotine, a substance known for its strong addictive properties, rapidly traverses to the central nervous system where it stimulates the release of dopamine, thereby eliciting sensations of pleasure. This affirmative reinforcement fosters the inclination to engage in smoking, thereby initiating the repetitive pattern.

The Role of Nicotine

Nicotine constitutes the primary psychoactive constituent found in tobacco products, wherein its impact on the brain is notably significant. It fosters the activation of neurotransmitters associated with feelings of pleasure and reward, thereby inducing a state of euphoria. Nevertheless, these advantages have a limited duration, prompting a perpetual cycle of desiring and consumption as individuals endeavor to replicate the gratifying encounters.

Physical and Psychological Components

The habit of smoking entails a combination of physiological and mental elements. The physiological aspect stems from the body's craving for nicotine. As nicotine levels decrease, individuals may experience withdrawal symptoms including irritability, anxiety, and strong urges, which compel them to pursue another cigarette as a means of alleviating the associated discomfort.

At the psychological level, smoking becomes intertwined with various emotions and occasions. It is commonly observed that smoking is often associated with the purpose of mitigating stress, promoting relaxation, or facilitating social interactions. These cognitive stimuli establish a profound and ingrained connection between cigarette consumption and one's emotional state of being, thereby rendering the cessation of this behavior quite challenging.

Social and Environmental Influences

Apart from the physiological and psychological factors, the smoking addiction is significantly influenced by social and environmental factors that are essential for its continuation. The normalization of smoking is influenced by factors such as peer influence, societal norms, and the portrayal of smoking in media. Furthermore, the existence of smoking stimuli, such as observing another individual engaging in smoking or encountering situations where smoking is prevalent, can elicit urges and cravings even in individuals who are actively striving to quit.

Liberation Blueprints: Approaches and Assistance

Acknowledging the extent of tobacco dependency is the initial stride towards liberation. Escaping this repetitive cycle necessitates the implementation of a multifaceted strategy:

Education: Developing a comprehensive understanding of the intricacies surrounding addiction empowers individuals to make informed choices. Acquiring knowledge on the physiological and psychological aspects of addiction aids in unraveling the enigma surrounding this behavior.

Nicotine Replacement Therapies (NRTs): NRTs, encompassing transdermal patches, chewing gums, and lozenges, administer controlled nicotine dosages to the body, thereby effectively mitigating withdrawal symptoms and facilitating a gradual reduction in nicotine dependence.

Behavioral Therapies: Cognitive-behavioral interventions enable individuals to discern stimuli, develop effective coping strategies, and substitute smoking-related behaviors with wholesome alternatives.

Support Networks: Comprised of close acquaintances, relatives, and organized support circles, these systems serve as a vital source of ongoing encouragement. Engaging in the mutual exchange of experiences and challenges with fellow individuals following a similar path fosters a sense of camaraderie and community.

The addiction to smoking is a multifaceted amalgamation of physiological, cognitive, and contextual factors. Gaining a comprehensive understanding of its intricacy is the primary prerequisite for emancipating oneself from its grasp. Through the integration of information, methodologies, and guidance, individuals have the ability to effectively navigate the challenges associated with withdrawal, reestablish their cognitive associations with smoking, and embark upon a journey towards a robust and smoke-free existence.

Overcoming the bonds of addiction is a profoundly transformative journey that requires unwavering commitment, yet the benefits—a profound sense of renewed wellness and enhanced physical condition—make the endeavor exceedingly worthwhile.

1 HOW THINGS ARE

The smoke cages

Allow me to present a candid assessment: while I could proceed by enumerating the adverse consequences attributed to smoking, it begs the question of its utility. I aim to present you with a novel perspective, one that is more comprehensive and lucid, regarding the issue at hand. In doing so, I will furnish you with substantial evidence, insights gleaned from past smokers, and firsthand accounts, all tailored to inspire contemplation centeredaround personal wellness. I am not present with the intention of delivering a lecture or reiterating commonly heard speeches. My objective is different: I aim to foster a discourse that introduces fresh insights, compelling you to contemplate the matter of smoking, as well as your existence, from an alternative vantage point. And subsequently, to be candid, did the widely disreputable lectures ever yield any positive outcomes? Based on my observations, I would assert that the answer is negative.

With what frequency do you observe individuals who smoke residing with parents who also engage in smoking activities? Often. Indeed, from a statistical standpoint, there exists a higher likelihood for offspring of smokers to develop the habit of smoking. This phenomenon is predicated upon the premise of emulation. While it is possible that this may not have been the scenario in your specific circumstances, it is important to note that in the majority of cases, I can provide reassurance that this holds true. On numerous occasions, I have encountered statements from parents or grandparents expressing their inability to put an end to a particular behavior, while simultaneously advocating against it, such as smoking. The insufficiency of this kind of resolve is readily apparent. The state imposes smoking restrictions in certain areas, advocates for anti-smoking initiatives, and simultaneously engages in the sale of tobacco products. In a manner reminiscent of the rapid pace of warnings accompanying medicinal products, the advertisement acknowledges the permissibility of "gambling" while emphasizing the prohibition of such activity among minors and the potential for it to lead to pathological addiction. Do you believe it does so with the intention of promoting the health and well-being of its citizens? Certainly not, otherwise it would not be able to offer specific "services" and "products". It is simply a means of legal safeguarding against potential liability claims. In the literary work entitled Assisting in the Cessation of Smoking? According to Fabio Lugoboni, the task at hand is more manageable than one might assume.

In Italy, there is variability in the prevalence of smoking among doctors. A few years ago, a study examining 983 pulmonology specialists found that 26.5% of them were engaged in smoking habits. Male doctors exhibit smoking rates that are equivalent to their counterparts in other professions, whereas female medical graduates surpass graduates from different fields in terms of smoking habits, constituting approximately 42% of the participants in a comprehensive study conducted on medical graduates hailing from Southern Italy. The United States, which has placed significant emphasis on combatting smoking as a primary healthcare objective, is a nation in which merely 2% of physicians engage in smoking, demonstrating a prevalence comparable to that of the United Kingdom. Furthermore, it is ensured that patients will not encounter a doctor belonging to this limited minority of smokers engaging in the act of lighting a cigarette.

Under such circumstances, it becomes a challenging task to discern the positive from the negative, the morally correct from the morally wrong, and the state of well-being from that of distress. Every day, we encounter a multitude of deceptive narratives that permeate our surroundings: ranging from persuasive advertisements, insidious and misleading information, and at times even from familial influences that instilllearned behaviors. These frequent encounters have led to a desensitization wherein the actions of others may appear acceptable, despite engaging in harmful behaviors that detriment ourselves and our society. In the present day, it is imperative that we anticipate transparency in situations where others may choose to withhold information from us. It is important to note that the more we are kept in a state of confusion and manipulation, the more susceptible we become to control, ultimately benefiting those who seek to exploit such circumstances for their own gain. Alternatively, we can opt to make discerning and deliberate choices, unaffected by manipulated desires. In addition to exercising our right to do so, this represents a form of agency we possess over our own lives. Smoking represents an indication, a manifestation of general discomfort, a form of warning. Furthermore, concurrently, it exacerbates the preexisting unstable psychological state. Subsequently, when incorporating the daily stress, the issue escalates akin to a snowball effect that transitions into an overwhelming avalanche downstream.

5

The pushback

M

My consistent habit of smoking persisted throughout my twenties without any obstacles, yet it was not until my thirties that I stumbled upon the revelation I am about to present to you. It may indeed appear sufficiently straightforward and evident, as it truly is; however, curiously,

I have never encountered any discourse regarding its pragmatic effectiveness as a cessation method for tobacco consumption. This approach evolved naturally for me over a period of time, and if you kindly indulge me, I will elucidate precisely why it is remarkably efficacious, devoid of any associated withdrawal symptoms. In the subsequent sections, I will additionally demonstrate techniques to expedite the procedure and customize it according to your requirements.

Therefore, I continued working in the construction industry, which afforded me the opportunity to travel to various destinations worldwide. I would transition between various job sites and work alongside different crews. It is conceivable that my respiratory system and other bodily organs were subjected to considerable harm, resulting not only from the influence of cigarettes but also from the consumption of alcohol and the overall lifestyle associated with working in the construction industry. My cough had intensified significantly, rendering me breathless every morning, even before beginning my day. My physical condition was deteriorating; it appeared that I was possibly venturing into perilous territory. Under no circumstances would I consent to undergoing a medical examination or any form of diagnostic procedure due to the apprehension I harbor regarding potential revelations.

Subsequently, on a certain day, possibly driven by need and reason, most likely both, I ceased the act of indulging in morning smoking. I refrained from beginning my first cigarette until the initial break, approximately at 10:30 a.m. Initially, it required some discipline, yet I discovered it to be quite manageable, and my respiratory system expressed gratitude for this decision. I suppose recognizing that the duration of time until I could proceed to illuminate alleviated the burden. The element that proved most beneficial in facilitating this adjustment was my decision to increase my daily walking routine and consistently carry a readily available bottle of water. I am of the opinion that these two alterations have assisted me in cultivating resilience and occupied my time. In the event that I experienced the inclination to smoke, I would engage in a brief stroll and have a beverage, even if it entailed merely circumnavigating the premises. These urges were of short duration, and to be honest, it did not pose significant difficulty to maintain self-control until the first interval materialized.

After several weeks, this developed into the customary routine and innate habit. I ceased the habit of instinctively reaching for cigarettes as my first action in the morning. I began experiencing an improvement in my well-being, and the regular occurrence of choking in the morning gradually subsided. A minimum of three cigarettes have been eliminated from my daily smoking habit, bringing about a sense of delight. I was gradually gaining advantage over my longstanding adversary, and it bestowed a gratifying sensation. I am uncertain about the duration between the initial stage toward success, but subsequently, I resolved to extend my period of abstaining from smoking until noon. This entailed an additional extension of two hours, resulting in the avoidance of at least three cigarettes. Once more, I discovered this task to be comparatively straightforward, and I began to sense that I had reached the culmination of my endeavors. I am now cognizant of the fact that I was traversing the path towards eliminating smoking from my existence. Subsequently, there was a gradual advancement characterized by two-hour increments. I dedicated a few months to successfully ceasing smoking during working hours, without feeling any significant pressure to expedite the process. I was immensely pleased to be making progress towards the correct path. It entailed a gradual and methodical course of action aimed at gradually reducing my dependence on them in the most effortless manner possible.

After refraining from smoking during the course of my workday, I noticed a further improvement in the level of ease. I proceeded to visit unfamiliar job sites, and the unfamiliar crew remained unaware of my smoking habit. This was highly enjoyable as there was a notable absence of individuals soliciting my participation in smoking or enticing me through other means. I persevered and gradually reduced my cigarette consumption to just one per day. Frankly speaking, I found myself content with this situation for several months. I was not fully prepared to completely discard them, and I experienced excellent physical well-being along with various other aspects. I must express a sense of pride in myself, as I have accomplished it all without enduring significant adversity. The consumption of alcoholic beverages posed significant adversities for me. Frequent were the occasions where I would revert to my previous habit of smoking during a session of imbibing, yet upon the arrival of the subsequent day, I resumed my practice of only indulging once, free from any regressions. The inclination to engage in smoking during the daytime had dissipated.

It was only upon receiving the news of my impending first child that I made the definitive choice to completely cease partaking in smoking. I recollect partaking in my final cigarette. The individual with whom I initially embarked upon this journey many years ago happened to be the very same cousin, although I was oblivious to its profound implications back then. A minimum duration of 25 years in bondage has come to an end. Amen.

As of the present moment, my firstborn has reached the age of eight, and I contemplate his growth as I reminisce about my own formative years. It is difficult to fathom that I was merely slightly older than him when I embarked on that harrowing path of despair. This is astounding, and it fills me with sorrow. Fortunately, I will not be the catalyst for his indulgence in smoking, and it is my sincere hope that the valuable insights I have gained will protect him and his younger sibling from enduring the same perils as their father. I am equally pleased to express my anticipation of being present throughout the process of witnessing my two sons' maturation into adulthood. I would have lacked the assurance to assert such a statement had I persisted along my former trajectory.

The Physiological And Psychological Hold Of Nicotine

Nicotine, an exceptionally potent alkaloid found in tobacco, ranks among the most habit-forming substances identified in human history. Due to its potent cravings and addictive qualities, cigarettes represent the primary psychoactive substance that a significant number of individuals persist in consuming. The influence of nicotine extends beyond mere physical addiction, encompassing psychological, social, and behavioral dimensions, rendering it a formidable adversary for individuals endeavoring to liberate themselves.

The activation of nicotinic acetylcholine receptors in the brain is triggered by nicotine, thus enabling it to exert its physiological influence. When nicotine binds to these receptors, which are integral to the brain's reward circuitry, it induces the secretion of neurotransmitters such as dopamine and norepinephrine. These neurotransmitters afford the individual immediate gratification by eliciting pleasurable sensations, heightening emotional state, and improving cognitive concentration. Due to the brain's progressive adaptation to these surges of neurotransmitters, a larger quantity of nicotine is required to produce the equivalent effect, thereby perpetuating the addiction.

The adverse physiological manifestations associated with nicotine addiction are profound. Individuals experiencing nicotine withdrawal may exhibit signs of agitation, anxiety, restlessness, and experience intense urges for nicotine. These symptoms serve to compound the challenge of abstaining from smoking or using other tobacco products. Nicotine withdrawal represents more than a fleeting inconvenience; rather, it serves as a testament to the profound physical dependence that nicotine has established within the body.

Nevertheless, nicotine's impacts extend beyond the realm of physiological effects. Moreover, it exerts a pronounced psychological influence on individuals. Numerous individuals who smoke possess enduring patterns and associations with smoking that transcend mere physical reliance. The practice of smoking becomes intertwined with routine tasks, interpersonal relationships, and alleviation of stress.

Nicotine frequently serves as a psychological aid for coping with life's challenges. Smoking has the potential to offer individuals a brief respite from feelings of tension, concern, or monotony. It serves as a reliable mechanism for many individuals to navigate their challenges. Equally challenging is the task of overcoming the physical desires as it is to detach oneself from this psychological bond. It could potentially be a daunting prospect for individuals who smoke to undertake the process of acquiring a new set of skills to manage their emotions and navigate their circumstances devoid of the perceived safety net provided by a cigarette.

Social factors contribute to the reinforcement of nicotine addiction. Smoking frequently serves as a communal experience, fostering camaraderie among individuals who indulge in this habit and forge connections during shared intervals for smoking. These social connections can potentially cultivate a sense of cohesion and inclusion that fortifies the behavior. Furthermore, in social gatherings such as bars or parties, smoking is frequently endorsed as a means of cultivating social connections, rendering it challenging to quit when constantly surrounded by smoking companions.

Profoundly ingrained behavioral patterns are likewise linked to nicotine dependency. Smokers establish smoking patterns encompassing diverse aspects such as their cigarette-holding method and specific instances and venues for smoking. Attempting to cease this behavior could disrupt one's established daily routines and lead to cognitive disorientation due to the deeply ingrained nature of these rituals. Escaping this psychological grip, deeply embedded in one's behavior and habits, can prove equally challenging as breaking free from the physical addiction.

The promotional efforts undertaken by the tobacco industry, historically aimed at glorifying smoking while downplaying its detrimental effects, serve to intensify the addictive power of nicotine. In spite of extensive public health initiatives and enhanced comprehension regarding the perils of smoking, tobacco corporations persist in focusing their efforts on susceptible populations, thereby perpetuating the cycle of addiction.

I

Introduction

In a bygone era, situated within the vicinity of undulating landscapes, resided an individual of the name James, within a quaint village. For an extensive period of time, James had been ensnared by an unyielding compulsion that significantly impacted the facets of his existence: the act of smoking. Every day, he would arise with the determination to quit, only to yield to the irresistible temptation of nicotine once more.

Nevertheless, on a momentous morning, when the sun adorned the sky with shades of tangerine and gilded tones, a transformation took place within James. He studied his own reflection in the mirror, noticing the visible creases on his face that were a stark testament to the adverse effects of smoking on his physical well-being.

With unwavering resolve to liberate himself from the clutches of addiction, James undertook a transformative quest of introspection and personal growth. He equipped himself with a comprehensive understanding of the adverse impacts of smoking, recognizing the gravity of the situation concerning his well-being.

James sought solace from his beloved acquaintances, who earnestly offered their steadfast support. He became a member of a support group, wherein he discovered comfort in listening to the narratives and victories of individuals who had traversed a similar journey.

With the aim of finding a simplified means to cease smoking, James adopted the utilization of nicotine replacement therapy, which facilitated the reduction of his cravings and ameliorated the symptoms associated with withdrawal. Additionally, he cultivated healthier practices, integrating physical activity and nourishing dietary choices into his daily regimen, resulting in a rejuvenated sense of vitality.

During the course of his journey, James encountered a plethora of obstacles. In times of heightened tension and susceptibility, the irresistible appeal of a cigarette continued to subtly beckon to him. Nevertheless, he persisted, keeping in mind the liberty he sought and the existence he longed to regain.

Over the course of several years, James persevered and ultimately achieved victory. Not only did he overcome his addiction, but he also underwent a profound journey of self-discovery in the process. James served as a source of inspiration for others, wholeheartedly recounting his journey to motivate and uplift individuals who faced challenges with smoking.

With a pleasant countenance and a revitalized sense of determination, James embraced his tobacco-free existence, appreciative of the fortitude and perseverance he had discovered within. Thus, the individual who was previously engulfed by the presence of smoke emerged as a symbol of encouragement, exemplifying the strength of resolve and the potential for personal growth.

Introduction:

Ceasing tobacco use presents a significant challenge that numerous individuals encounter during their lifetime. The highly addictive characteristics of nicotine, coupled with the habitual elements of smoking, can create a sense of overwhelming difficulty. Nevertheless, discovering a convenient approach to cease smoking is not solely achievable but has the potential to greatly enhance your physical health, sense of well-being, and overall standard of living.

Numerous scientific studies have uncovered the adverse repercussions associated with smoking on human health, encompassing escalated vulnerabilities to malignancies, cardiovascular conditions, respiratory complications, and premature aging. Cessation of smoking not only mitigates these health hazards but also presents immediate advantages, including enhanced pulmonary function, elevated levels of vitality, and a heightened perception of taste and smell.

Although the path to achieving a smoke-free life can appear daunting, it is crucial to acknowledge that you are not solitary in undertaking this endeavor. Numerous individuals have effectively ceased the habit of smoking, and by employing appropriate tactics and receiving adequate assistance, one can also liberate oneself from the clutches of nicotine dependency.

In this comprehensive guide, we aim to delve into a multitude of strategies and approaches that can facilitate the process of smoking cessation for individuals. We will present a thorough overview of strategies proven to be efficacious in smoking cessation, encompassing an in-depth analysis of nicotine addiction and associated withdrawal symptoms, as well as an examination of modalities such as nicotine replacement therapy, pharmaceutical interventions, and behavioral techniques.

Moreover, we will explore the significance of adopting lifestyle modifications in order to facilitate your progress towards achieving a smoke-free state. Adopting a nutritious dietary regimen, engaging in consistent physical activity, implementing effective stress reduction methods, and abstaining from smoking triggers will all serve as pivotal factors in achieving favorable outcomes.

In addition, we will also tackle the obstacles that might arise during your journey and furnish you with strategies to maintain your determination while effectively managing and surmounting the desire to smoke. The topics of relapse prevention strategies and the importance of seeking professional assistance when necessary will also be addressed.

Please bear in mind that ceasing the habit of smoking is an ongoing progression that necessitates unwavering dedication, persistence, and assistance. By acquiring information, embracing efficient methodologies, and implementing lifestyle modifications, you will enhance the likelihood of effectively ceasing smoking and reestablishing mastery over your life and well-being.

Now, let us commence this voyage hand in hand, exploring the efficacious methods to cease smoking, empowering you to enact constructive transformations and embrace a life free from tobacco.

Efficacious Cognitive-Behavioral Therapy Techniques for the Management of Cravings:

1. Thought Documentation: Maintain a record of your thoughts to monitor your cravings. Please document the inciting incident, your cognitive processes, affective responses, and the resulting consequences. Conduct an assessment to determine the veracity or distortion of your thoughts.

2. Socratic Inquiry: Engage in the practice of Socratic inquiry to critically examine your thoughts. Kindly inquire within oneself, "Does this thought align with reality?" Can I be provided with

substantiating evidence? What advice would I offer to an individual facing a comparable predicament?

3. Employing the technique of decatastrophizing enables one to gain a more rational and balanced outlook when faced with an overpowering craving. Consider the following inquiry: "Ponder this question: 'What are the potential adverse outcomes if I refrain from smoking at this moment?'"

4. Utilization of Diversionary Techniques: Employ diversionary activities to occupy oneself when faced with a craving. Shift your attention by engaging in activities such as reading, solving puzzles, or indulging in a leisure activity that brings you pleasure.

5. Employing Constructive Internal Dialogue: Offset cravings by using positive self-talk. Reinforce your determination by recalling the rationales behind your decision to cease smoking,

your advancements in this endeavor, and the advantages associated with leading a smoke-free lifestyle.

6. Imagery: Employ the technique of imagery to vividly envision yourself triumphantly conquering cravings. Envision yourself skillfullymaneuvering through stimuli and triumphantly prevailing.

7. Behavior Modification: Substituting the habit of smoking with a more beneficial behavior. In the event of experiencing a craving, it is advised to engage in a vigorous walk, consume water, or engage in deep breathing exercises.

8. Engage in the practice of journaling as a means to delve into one's thoughts and emotions. Take time to contemplate your achievements, obstacles encountered, and successful approaches that have yielded results.

Consistency and Patience:

The application of cognitive-behavioral therapy techniques necessitates the cultivation of proficiency and perseverance. By consistently implementing these strategies, you will enhance your aptitude in managing urges and rewiring cognitive patterns. With the passage of time, you will observe a transformation in your perception of cravings, accompanied by a newfound sensation of mastery.

Empowering Lasting Change:

By integrating cognitive-behavioral therapy (CBT) techniques into your approach for managing cravings, you are enabling yourself to liberate from the clutches of intense urges. You are fostering resilience, augmenting your self-awareness, and constructing a repertoire of skills that will support you not only in your journey of cessation, but also in the entirety of your life. By actively reformulating your thoughts and reactions, you are cultivating enduring transformation and edging nearer to a future characterized by your resilience and a lifestyle free from smoking.

Seven: Unveiling Your Individual Motivational Catalyst.

I would like to present the question to you: "What is the underlying motivation behind your desire to quit smoking?" This will help you discover your individual motivating factor. A compelling rationale that holds significant sway, particularly when it concerns individuals dear to you. Utilize this phrase in your internal dialogue as a mnemonic prompt to be periodically reflected upon during the course of this endeavor.

The majority of individuals throughout their lifespan tend to prioritize the well-being and welfare of others over their own. If you are able to discern a rationale, an underlying rationale, exemplified by the desire to quit smoking for the benefit of others such as a spouse, children, or parents, engaging in such actions creates an emotional bond and strengthens your motivational drive.

When we integrate our loved ones into our why factor, it serves as an intrinsic impetus, a powerful motivating force, to accomplish the intended outcomes. For instance, a specific individual, who happens to be the father of a child, made the decision to cease smoking as a result of his son's asthma affliction. In essence, his motivation to quit smoking derived from the desire to prioritize his son's well-being. One can undertake this action not only for the sake of their parents, but also for the benefit of their children, their spouse, or any individual.

Within my Coaching & Training enterprise, the driving force behind my actions and aspirations rests upon the fundamental objective of extending oneself, providing aid, and imparting assistance to a significant number of individuals. Equally important is the desire to elicit a sense of pride within my Father and Parents, thereby solidifying my purpose. Whenever the demands of my job become overwhelming or burdensome, I take a reflective moment to inquire, 'Am I still driven by the desire to make a substantial impact on numerous individuals?' Consistently, my response resounds with an unequivocal affirmation - 'Undoubtedly, yes.' Once more, I find myself contemplating, "Do I still desire to earn the pride of my father/parents?" The response remains resolutely, "Certainly, affirmative." And this imbues me with the intrinsic determination, impetus, internal energy, and fervor required to successfully complete the endeavors I have undertaken.

For instance, the process of authoring and making this book available to the public was fraught with challenges, necessitating substantial amounts of time invested in editing, revising, and meticulously reviewing the content over the course of several days. At certain points, I came close to relinquishing my efforts. I promptly called to mind my core motivation and dutifully finalized this task.

Further Justifications for Ceasing Tobacco Consumption (in conjunction with those you have already considered)

At this point, it is expected that you have discerned a minimum of two sentimental justifications for coming across this book - motivations that explain your desire to cease smoking. If you have not done so already, I kindly request you to momentarily halt your activities and engage in deep introspection. If the underlying rationale is not adequately identified, my proposed resolution will be rendered ineffective. I apologize, however, there is no alternative solution to bypassing that particular stage.

Should you possess a written record of your sentimental motives, or if they exist within your mental realm, I am inclined to furnish you with several additional rationales - ones rooted in logic - pertaining to the cessation of smoking.

Your health

You are already familiar with this information. One of the utmost considerations that ought to be made pertains to the paramount importance of one's personal well-being. It is imperative that you cease the habit of smoking in order to enhance your overall well-being and significantly increase your prospects of attaining a prolonged lifespan.

Cessating tobacco consumption alleviates your susceptibility to ailments, including but not limited to cardiovascular disease, lung, liver, oral and throat malignancies, respiratory complications, and impaired fertility.

Furthermore, upon cessation of smoking, your sensory system undergoes a recovery process. Food becomes more flavorful, your olfactory senses become heightened, your discolored teeth and fingernails regain their nutritional balance, and your hair, clothing, and breath emit a pleasant fragrance.

It's an all-round transformation.

Your loved ones

Your loved ones may encompass individuals for whom you hold romantic feelings, acquaintances, conversational companions, infatuations, or trusted confidants. Occasionally, they possess the ability to incite a desire for greater fulfillment in one's existence. When considering the cherished presence of your loved ones, their profound concern for your well-being and unwavering desire to safeguard your presence in their lives, along with the abundant affection and support they have bestowed upon you, it is imperative that you aspire to renounce smoking.

Your concentration level

When engaging in smoking, one's attention becomes directed towards the single objective of appeasing the desire for nicotine. Conversely, when you cease smoking, your level of focus corresponds to the entirety of your physique. Cessation of smoking aids in restoring one's concentration to a normal state.

With that being stated, I am of the opinion that good health serves as a form of riches, and one should seriously consider factors such as sound mental well-being, familial ties, and cherished relationships when making the decision to cease smoking.

Ineffective Approaches to Smoking Cessation and the Reason Behind the Lack of Success with Alternative Measures

Discontinuing tobacco use without a substitute strategy

In order to relinquish any habitual behavior, it is imperative to possess a substitution. This aids in the complete cessation of such a habit, ensuring no subsequent recurrence. Suppose your aim is to curtail impulsive purchasing. In order to achieve this, it is necessary to substitute it with the practice of creating a comprehensive list. Therefore, prior to embarking on a shopping excursion, it is imperative that you carefully devise a list and consistently adhere to it. Similarly, cessation of smoking cannot be achieved without a suitable substitute for the smoking habit.

Rather than simply ceasing the habit, individuals should consider replacing smoking with alternative practices like exercise, meditation, and engaging in mindfulness activities. This will aid you in ceasing smoking and cultivating greater determination.

Strategically cutting down

One incorrect approach to cease smoking is to employ a strategic reduction method, such as opting to diminish the frequency of smoking occasions per week from seven to four. While it may appear to be an appealing strategy, it often proves ineffective due to its tendency to enable relapse. I must express that it is a rational approach; thus far, each decrease in the consumption of cigarette sticks has proven to diminish harm. Nonetheless, the most effective means of permanently ceasing smoking is by relinquishing the habit altogether.

To achieve optimal results, it is recommended to eliminate smoking entirely, rather than attempting a gradual reduction.

Strategically cutting down

One incorrect approach to cease smoking is to employ strategic reduction, such as making the deliberate decision to decrease smoking occurrences per week from seven to four. While the concept may initially appear promising, it has been observed that this approach is seldom effective as it allows for the possibility of regression. I must express that this is an acceptable methodology. Thus far, each diminution in the quantity of cigarette sticks has proven to diminish the associated risks.

However, the most effective means to permanently refrain from smoking is to relinquish the habit altogether.

It is advised to completely cease smoking rather than gradually reduce it, as this approach yields better results.

Using hypnotherapy

The American Cancer Society (ACS) contends that insufficient evidence exists to substantiate the effectiveness of hypnotherapy. Hypnotherapy is a form of adjunctive healthcare that leverages the power of the mind's imagination to assist in overcoming maladaptive behaviors, as well as alleviating discomfort associated with stress and anxiety.

Rather than indulging in imaginative thoughts, it is advisable to substitute them with techniques such as breathing exercises and engaging in mindfulness activities. This effectively addresses your nicotine cravings.

Using herbs

One of the issues surrounding herbal products is the dearth of regulations pertaining to their utilization, thereby increasing the likelihood of unforeseen complications at an accelerated pace. You have conditioned both your mind and body to rely on nicotine for functioning, thus it is not advisable to attempt reprogramming through the arbitrary use of different herbs. Indeed, should one fail to exercise caution, they will be exposing themselves to a range of additional health ailments.

Smoking operates on a scientifically verifiable basis, influencing the body in discernible ways. Therefore, there exists a definitive scientific knowledge on how to successfully cease an activity. Therefore, in lieu of employing herbs and unregulated dietary supplements, it is recommended to opt for scientifically supported remedies and augment your diet with fruits and vegetables in order to purify your system.

C. Developing Continual Motivation and Commemorating Achievements to Maintain a Smoke-Free Lifestyle

Maintaining motivation and commemorating milestones are imperative for achieving sustained long-term success. The following guidelines can assist in maintaining one's motivation:

Establish fresh objectives: Consistently establish new aims in order to sustain motivation and direct your attention towards the favorable elements of your life free from smoking. Strive for individual accomplishments such as enhanced physical well-being, acquisition of novel expertise, or engagement in meaningful leisure activities.

Engage in introspection regarding the advantages: Continuously prompt yourself of the positive outcomes you have personally witnessed as a result of ceasing your smoking habit. Enhanced physical well-being, amplified vitality, and heightened overall state of wellness serve as compelling sources of inspiration.

Acknowledge achievements: Recognize and commemorate significant milestones in your journey towards being smoke-free, be it completing a week, a month, or even a year since you quit. Indulge in something significant or commemorate your achievements with dear ones to acknowledge your advancement and fortify your dedication.

Embrace a circle of positivity: Cultivate relationships with individuals who wholeheartedly advocate for and endorse your smoke-free lifestyle. Refrain from engaging with contexts or individuals that may hinder your endeavors, and instead actively search for sources of constructive influence.

Engage in self-care practices: Give importance to activities that enhance one's overall well-being. Ensure you obtain sufficient rest, consume a well-rounded and nutritious diet, partake in consistent physical exercise, and engage in activities that provide contentment and relaxation.

By integrating these strategies into your daily routine, you can efficiently manage cravings, thwart relapse, and uphold your smoke-free status.

In the final chapter, we will provide a comprehensive overview of key points, present concluding remarks to motivate you, and instill in you a sense of optimism and satisfaction as you embrace a smoke-free lifestyle.

The Subjugation Of Minds: Unveiling The Influence Of Advertising And Societal Conformity In The Promotion Of Smoking

Smoking is a pervasive behavior with consequences that extend to a global scale, impacting millions of individuals across the globe. Although curiosity or peer pressure may be responsible for some individuals initiating smoking, a significant number of people develop this habit due to the deliberate and persistent influence of advertising and marketing. Throughout its history, the tobacco industry has effectively employed advertising tools to foster the allure of smoking and cultivate a favorable perception of this habit among consumers.

The tobacco industry, via advertising, has successfully established smoking as a socially desirable and alluring behavior. Advertisements frequently portray smokers as individuals who exude self-assurance, physical allure, and achievements, wherein smoking is positioned as a symbol of elevated social standing and personal autonomy. This communication is specifically aimed at the youth demographic, who exhibit higher susceptibility to the impact of promotional content and are more inclined towards developing enduring behavioral patterns.

The influence of advertisements on smoking behaviors transcends solely the youth cohort. Grown individuals also exhibit responses to the conveyed messages and imagery found in tobacco advertisements, frequently in an unconscious manner. The continual presentation of affirmative smoking images can engender a potent and enduring cognitive connection that associates smoking with desirability and social acceptability. This may result in a self-perpetuating cycle, wherein individuals persist in smoking due to their perception that it is socially sanctioned behavior.

Aside from advertising, social mores also play a noteworthy role in facilitating the prevalence of smoking. In numerous cultures, smoking is perceived as a socially sanctioned behavior, whereby individuals who smoke are frequently regarded as integrated members of a unified community. This phenomenon has the potential to foster a feeling of affiliation and individuality among smokers, thereby impeding their cessation efforts due to the apprehension of severing their social ties.

The influence exerted by advertising and social norms in propagating smoking extends beyond the individual sphere. At the collective level, these influences can foster a smoking culture that is deeply rooted and resistant to change. Governments and public health institutions encounter notable obstacles in their endeavors to diminish smoking rates due to the formidable opposition posed by well-entrenched cultural practices and the influential sway of the tobacco industry.

To summarize, smoking frequently becomes a habit as a result of extensive advertisement and societal conditioning.

The tobacco sector has a lengthy track record of utilizing advertising to cultivate a favorable perception of smoking, while societal conventions have perpetuated the practice by deeming it socially permissible. The convergence of these influences can give rise to a pervasive smoking culture that is deeply entrenched and resistant to transformation, posing significant obstacles for individuals in their cessation efforts. In order to significantly decrease smoking rates, it is imperative to tackle the underlying factors contributing to smoking, such as the impact of promotional campaigns and societal expectations. This necessitates a continuous and synchronized endeavor on the part of public health agencies, authorities, and localities, in order to cultivate a societal mindset that prioritizes the significance of health and wellness over the glorification of smoking.

One: Gaining Insight into the Difficulties Associated with Smoking Cessation

Introduction:

We extend our warm congratulations to you for embarking on the initial stage towards a well-being-oriented existence, completely free from tobacco use! The act of abandoning smoking is truly admirable, yet it should be acknowledged that this endeavor may present certain hardships along the way. In the following chapter, we shall delve into the various obstacles that one may face when attempting to quit smoking and present insightful strategies to successfully surmount them.

Section 1: The Physiological Obstacles

1.1 The Overwhelming Grip of Nicotine Addiction.

The psychoactive substance known as nicotine, which is present in tobacco products, exerts a profound influence on the functioning of your central nervous system and physiological well-being. Over a duration of time, the act of smoking ultimately results in a condition known as nicotine dependence, thereby rendering the cessation process challenging. Upon cessation of smoking, the human body experiences a strong desire for nicotine, which subsequently manifests as withdrawal symptoms including irritability, anxiety, restlessness, and heightened cravings.

Having a comprehensive understanding of the potency of nicotine addiction is vital in order to surmount these physiological obstacles.

1.2 Managing Withdrawal Symptoms

As you embark on the process of smoking cessation, you might encounter a range of withdrawal symptoms. The aforementioned symptoms may manifest in a diversified manner among individuals, yet typically encompass episodes of headaches, exhaustion, impaired cognitive focus, heightened appetite, and fluctuations in mood. Effectively managing and dealing with these symptoms is imperative in order to achieve a successful cessation of smoking.

Section 2: The Psychological and Emotional Difficulties

2.1 The Influence of Psychological Triggers and Associations

Smoking frequently becomes entangled with particular circumstances, feelings, and routines. It can be linked to alleviating stress, engaging in social interactions, or serving as a means of managing specific emotions. The presence of these psychological triggers may present formidable obstacles in the process of smoking cessation. It is of utmost importance to ascertain the factors that activate your response and explore alternative approaches to effectively manage these occurrences or emotional states in order to emancipate yourself from the psychological associations related to tobacco.

2.2 Emotional Roller Coaster

Cessation of smoking can evoke a range of emotions, encompassing anxiety, frustration, sadness, and irritability. The process could become increasingly demanding as nicotine withdrawal intensifies these emotions. Recognizing that these fluctuations in emotions are inherent to the process of quitting and crucially, establishing effective coping strategies to navigate them, is imperative for achieving sustained success.

3: Societal and Environmental Dilemmas

3.1 Conformity and Persuasion in a Social Context

Quitting smoking can be difficult due to the interpersonal implications associated with its social nature. The impact of social influence, specifically the pressures exerted by peers and close relatives who are smokers, may prove to be a hindrance in diligently adhering to your cessation strategy. Developing effective approaches to navigate social situations in which smoking is common and seeking assistance from close confidants are crucial measures in conquering these obstacles.

3.2 Environmental Triggers

The surrounding physical environment has the potential to serve as a catalyst for engaging in smoking behavior. The presence of locations, items, or activities pertaining to smoking can potentially rekindle desires and enticements. Having an awareness of your environment and identifying strategies to adjust or sidestep potential triggers can greatly improve your likelihood of maintaining a tobacco-free lifestyle.

Conclusion:

Gaining a comprehensive understanding of the difficulties associated with tobacco cessation is imperative in adequately preparing oneself mentally and emotionally. By recognizing and taking into account the various obstacles that exist on physical, psychological, and environmental levels, you enhance your ability to triumph over them. Please be mindful that ceasing the habit of smoking requires a continuous process, wherein overcoming each obstacle propels you towards a more harmonious and tobacco-free existence. In the forthcoming sections, we will delve into efficacious methodologies, organic remedies, and pragmatic recommendations to facilitate your cessation of smoking and commence a gratifying, tobacco-free trajectory.

Three: Preparing for Cessation

A triumphant endeavor to cease a particular habit necessitates meticulous groundwork, strategizing, and unwavering dedication. In the subsequent chapter, we will investigate the indispensable measures to undertake as you prepare for your pursuit of a smoke-free lifestyle.

Establishing a designated cessation date

Selecting a cessation date is an essential milestone in your pursuit of smoking cessation. This designated date serves as a tangible objective, aiding in one's psychological readiness for the impending challenge. When determining the date on which you plan to cease your activities, it is advisable to take into account the following factors:

Select a date that is in relative proximity, so as to avoid the risk of diminishing motivation or experiencing a change of heart.

Refrain from choosing a date that aligns with a significant life occasion or a time marked by elevated levels of stress.

Take into consideration selecting a date that holds personal significance, such as a birthday or anniversary, in order to enhance your motivation to cease the habit.

After selecting your designated cessation date, make a note of it on your calendar and inform individuals in your social and professional networks, such as friends, family, and colleagues, to ensure personal responsibility.

Establishing a framework for assistance

Having a robust network of support can greatly enhance your likelihood of successfully ceasing smoking. Prior to your designated date of resignation, invest effort into developing a support network consisting of individuals who can offer words of motivation, empathy, and direction during the course of your endeavor. Your support network may consist of:

Individuals within your social circle, including close relatives and trusted acquaintances, who offer unwavering encouragement towards your resolve to cease participating in a particular activity.

Peers or associates who can provide motivation and support during working hours.

Ex-smokers who have effectively quit and are able to offer valuable guidance and perspectives.

Communal networks, whether physical or virtual, that afford you the opportunity to establish meaningful connections with individuals encountering analogous hurdles.

Healthcare practitioners, including physicians and therapists, who are capable of offering assistance in the form of medication or behavioral therapies to facilitate the process of cessation.

Identifying smoking triggers

As elucidated in 2, the stimuli that prompt smoking can encompass various facets, namely emotional, social, or environmental factors. It is imperative to recognize one's individual triggers in order to devise effective methods for their management. To identify your triggers:

Maintain a comprehensive record of your smoking habits for a minimum of one week prior to your designated cessation date. Please document in this journal every instance of cigarette consumption, including the precise time, as well as the corresponding circumstances such as the setting, emotional disposition, and individuals present.

Examine your journal entries to discern recurring patterns and shared catalysts for your smoking tendencies.

Creating a cessation strategy.

The implementation of a comprehensive cessation plan can effectively navigate individuals through the difficulties associated with ceasing the habit of smoking. Your plan should include:

Your designated cessation date along with a written pledge to cease.

A compilation of recognized stimuli that can prompt smoking behaviors, accompanied by a set of tactics to effectively cope with them, such as engaging in alternative activities and employing stress reduction techniques.

A strategy for managing cravings, such as implementing nicotine replacement therapy (NRT) or participating in a diverting pursuit.

A strategy for the management of withdrawal symptoms, encompassing potential treatments such as pharmacotherapy, relaxation methodologies, or physical activity.

An assortment of supportive resources encompassing individuals within one's social network such as friends and family, dedicated support groups, as well as healthcare professionals and practitioners.

CHAPTERS 2

Strategies for Ceasing Tobacco Use

If the prominent billboard in Los Angeles, serving as a cautionary display against smoking, has failed to captivate your attention or persuade you to renounce the habit. According to experts, a predominant precipitating factor leading to smoking cessation is an unforeseen inadvertent consequence or an emotional response.

The stages for quitting smoking are comprehensively outlined on the smokerfree.gov website, specifically on the page titled "Basic Steps" (http://www.smokefree.gov/guide/basic steps.html).

S = Select a designated cessation date.

Inform your loved ones and colleagues of your intention to resign. A = Exercise awareness and make appropriate preparations for the challenges that will arise upon cessation. Resolutely banish tobacco products and cigarettes from your residence, automobile, place of employment, as well as any vehicles.

T = Engage in a conversation with your physician regarding the acquisition of assistance in smoking cessation.

Now, let us proceed with delineating the stages using our framework.

Prior knowledge of the life event that served as a catalyst for your decision to quit smoking is required. It is crucial to acknowledge this information as it will lead to a profound transformation in your life, creating a sense of rebirth.

Our recommendation is for you to confide in a trusted individual, such as a close friend or family member, regarding your intentions. Additionally, we contend that a forceful eruption is the sole feasible course of action. The choice to relinquish the cigarette from your grasp might have been influenced by a deeply personal and emotive context; it may have been partially consumed or otherwise. following the last puff. Please refrain from exhibiting concern or worry about the potential wastage or misuse of the remaining package, I implore you. The monetary impact of the discarded cigarette is inconsequential when compared to the substantial cost savings you will experience in the days to come as a result of your pioneering decision.

A sophisticated approach to decision-making and notifying the audience involves the option of rescheduling the event, even in the event of minor complications. It is important to be aware that there may be individuals who will advise against quitting smoking, possibly due to feelings of envy or a fear of experiencing social isolation as a result of losing a smoking companion. The only advantage of articulating such a declaration lies in its ability to exert heightened expectations upon oneself in order to meet one's duties.

In an environment characterized by high smoking prevalence, who will duly prompt you with reminders of your obligations and the possibility of embarrassment, given that the failures of the committed individuals largely go unnoticed? Hence, we implore you to refrain from making unfounded judgments.

Based on the online edition of BBC News, it was discovered through interviews conducted by researchers at University College London with over 1,900 smokers and ex-smokers regarding their cessation efforts that approximately two-thirds of those who abruptly quit achieved enduring success for a minimum of six months. This stands in stark contrast to the mere fraction of individuals who meticulously planned and strategized their quitting approaches, finding success in less than half of these cases.

Another critical factor is the solace that the smoker derives from the broader community. As though this represents the pivotal answer to the urgent question of why they persist in smoking, their inclination to justify their choice to initiate smoking intensifies. Smoking is an undesirable behavior, and it is our intention to clearly convey this message.

At times, individuals may engage in smoking out of habit, regardless of their lack of affection for it. Some individuals, even when confronted with the challenging query "why do you engage in smoking?", have uttered highly conventional phrases such as "just because" in their response.

The cigarette that remains unfinished or the packet that has been only partially consumed, though, might have been discarded in a manner that exudes a sense of romance. What follows is what? Due to the dispersal of nicotine throughout the central nervous system, causing disruption to the entire physiological system, it will not readily relinquish its grip on an individual as easily as it did during initial exposure. When one experiences psychological repercussions due to an inherent impatience to resume the current task. Should you seek medical assistance promptly upon quitting smoking, healthcare professionals will provide guidance and support, as well as offer recommendations for further actions and potentially prescribe suitable medication, if deemed necessary.

We are of the opinion that victory in the game can be achieved if you manage to abstain from engaging with the cigarette corner shop for a few hours. Might I suggest considering a visit to a cinema or leisurely park as a means to occupy your time while your prompt decision-making ability is operational? To alleviate tedium, you might also opt to accompany your cherished companion to a smoke-free dining establishment. When evening descends, you arrive at your residence empty-handed, having refrained from acquiring a cigarette, and proceed to undertake the act

Rather than hastily retreating to bed, it is advisable to exercise control over your restless thoughts. Kindly avoid strolling on the balcony, particularly considering that you were previously smoking in that area.

A number of individuals have acquired the practice of maintaining a plentiful supply of cigarettes at their workplaces or residences in preparation for unexpected situations. If you pertain to this practical cohort, please be reminded to promptly discard your entire stock into the waste receptacle upon entering your bedroom. Convince yourself that reconstructing a stock once more tomorrow will not consume significant time, but grant me the opportunity to undertake it at least until tomorrow morning!

Individuals who engage in smoking have been observed to display a preference for the visual perception of smoke rather than that of flame. Their sole intention is to observe the ascent of smoke rings, henceforth they have positioned themselves within a chamber that is devoid of any illumination. As per the report authored by VasudevanNampoothiri, the Vice-Principal of the Government Ayurveda College in Thiruvananthapuram, which was published on May 31, 2004, in The Hindu. You are required to make a selection between the flame and the fumes, providing a thorough justification for your preference.

When a cigarette undergoes combustion, only the observer can perceive the smoke rings. However, if a flame ignites within an individual, the rings generated by the dissipated energy become apparent to all, as they will inevitably reverberate off their surroundings.

Allow the first light of dawn to herald the arrival of a new day and infuse your life with revitalizing energy. We assure you that the sensation of dizziness will subside, and in due course, you will derive revitalization from the Sun, thereby replenishing your bodily and mental vigor.

Draw a long breath. It is essential to bear in mind that energy therapies such as Ayurveda and Qigong, among others, should be duly considered. Regard the early sunlight as a magnificent instrument of restoration. In the ancient city of Rome, renowned for its rich historical heritage and being a cradle of world civilizations, heliotherapy and chromotherapy have emerged as the predominant modalities of treatment. Two decades hence, one may yet experience the enduring vitality that flows within them!

Best wishes to you!

Understanding Nicotine Addiction

Nicotine dependency exerts a formidable influence over countless individuals globally, rendering it one of the most arduous addictions to surmount. In order to effectively initiate a prosperous endeavor to cease smoking, it is imperative to deeply delve into the intricate mechanisms and consequential manifestations of nicotine dependence, thereby obtaining a thorough comprehension of its profound repercussions on the physiological and psychological aspects of the individual.

The Scientific Explanation of Nicotine Dependency

Nicotine, an inherent constituent present in tobacco, serves as the primary addictive agent in cigarettes and various other tobacco derivatives. Upon entering the body, nicotine expeditiously reaches the brain and attaches itself to specific receptors, thereby eliciting the discharge of neurotransmitters like dopamine. The subsequent release of dopamine generates pleasurable sensations, thereby facilitating the gratifying outcomes that fortify the cycle of addiction.

The Impact of Nicotine on the Physiological and Cognitive Functions

Nicotine addiction not only exerts an impact on the brain, but also engenders a plethora of effects on the physical well-being. When one breathes in, nicotine causes the constriction of blood vessels, elevates heart rate, and augments blood pressure, thereby exerting pressure on the cardiovascular system. Gradually, the cumulative exposure to nicotine can result in the formation of tolerance, thereby requiring increased dosages to attain comparable outcomes.

In addition to its physiological consequences, nicotine addiction profoundly affects the cognitive and affective faculties. Numerous individuals who smoke often establish a psychological dependence due to their association of smoking with alleviation of stress, fostering of relaxation, or augmentation of concentration. This fusion of nicotine dependency with emotional and psychological elements can render the cessation process notably more formidable.

Disrupting the Pattern of Substance Dependency

In order to emancipate oneself from the clutches of nicotine dependence, it is imperative to comprehend the very cycle that perpetuates its hold. The addiction cycle generally comprises of four phases: inception, sustenance, recurrence, and abstinence.

Inception transpires when an individual initially engages in smoking, frequently motivated by a sense of curiosity, influence from peers, or a yearning for social acceptance. As smoking persists, the maintenance phase ensues, marked by the habitual consumption of nicotine in order to alleviate cravings and sustain the addictive cycle.

Recurrence, a frequent phenomenon in substance dependency, denotes the resumption of smoking following a period of abstention. Recurrences can be induced by a plethora of factors, encompassing stress, social circumstances, or the accessibility of cigarettes. It is of great significance to perceive relapses as obstacles rather than defeats, leveraging them as valuable learning experiences to fortify your determination and cultivate efficient mechanisms for coping.

The act of discontinuing smoking poses a considerable obstacle for individuals.

Upon nicotine intake, the human body undergoes a process of adaptation. Abrupt discontinuation or decrease in nicotine consumption can result in the manifestation of withdrawal symptoms. These symptoms may encompass a spectrum of manifestations, including but not limited to irritability, anxiety, diminished ability to concentrate, heightened cravings, and augmented appetite. Having knowledge and making necessary preparations regarding withdrawal symptoms can enable individuals to anticipate and successfully handle them while undergoing the cessation process.

Overcoming Nicotine Addiction

Addressing nicotine addiction necessitates the adoption of a comprehensive, multidimensional strategy. To begin with, it is imperative to acknowledge that nicotine addiction is a medical ailment, rather than a deficiency of resolve or personal incompetence. This change in viewpoint has the potential to enable individuals to approach the act of quitting with a sense of self-compassion, thereby actively seeking out suitable support and treatment.

The cessation techniques employed can differ, thus rendering ineffective those approaches that prove fruitful for some individuals but inconsequential for others. Nicotine replacement therapy (NRT), such as transdermal patches, chewing gum, or medicated lozenges, can effectively alleviate withdrawal symptoms by dispensing nicotine in a regulated manner, which aids in the gradual reduction of dependence. Additional pharmacological treatments, such as bupropion or varenicline, may be recommended to facilitate smoking cessation.

Psychological and emotional facets of nicotine addiction can be effectively addressed through counseling or support groups, which serve as indispensable behavioral interventions. These interventions offer direction, affirmation, and a secure environment for the examination of the underlying factors behind smoking, the creation of effective coping mechanisms, and the reception of sustained assistance during the process of quitting.

Gaining a comprehensive comprehension of nicotine addiction is an essential stride in the endeavor to cease smoking. Through acquiring knowledge of the scientific aspects underlying the addictive qualities of nicotine, acknowledging its impact on both the physical and psychological faculties, and attaining a comprehensive comprehension of the cycle of addiction, individuals can embark upon the process of quitting with a well-informed approach, resolute determination, and a cogent awareness of the obstacles they are likely to encounter. Equipped with this comprehension, coupled with efficacious cessation techniques and assistance networks, individuals can liberate themselves from the clutches of nicotine dependency and welcome a more salubrious, tobacco-free prospect.

While comprehensive comprehension of the scientific underpinnings of nicotine addiction is imperative, effectively emancipating oneself from its clutches necessitates a multi-dimensional strategy that encompasses the physical, psychological, and sociological facets of addiction. Through the implementation of a comprehensive approach, individuals can enhance their prospects of achieving long-term success in the cessation of cigarette consumption.

Initiate the First Phase - Schedule a Date

Commence your efforts to comprehend and accept the notion that you will cease the habit of smoking. This process commences by establishing a specific date. I would suggest scheduling your appointment at least 5 to 6 weeks in advance, preferably for a specific time, such as 12:00 AM midnight. It may appear rather daunting to designate a specific date on the calendar signifying the moment you entirely renounce smoking – nevertheless, embrace this decision wholeheartedly! Rest assured, by taking this initial stride, you shall witness the emergence of fortitude and self-assurance in due course.

There exists both a psychological and practical rationale behind this course of action, which you shall discover firsthand. After designating a specific date, it is essential that you adopt the practice of consciously acknowledging each cigarette smoked thereafter. Take a moment to reflect upon the cigarette in hand, reminding yourself that its significance is fleeting. Recognize that by quitting, you are breaking free from the grip of addiction, ultimately rendering these cigarettes unnecessary in your journey towards a smoke-free life. This process contributes to the mental preparation needed to cease smoking and embark upon a new characterized by enhanced liberty and consequently, a deepened sense of contentment.

Please be mindful that every instance of smoking moving forward should be accompanied by the silent repetition of these words in your mind, marking the commencement of your journey towards becoming a complete non-smoker. This, in and of itself, exerts a profound subconscious influence that gradually severs the bonds linking you to the smoking addiction.

Proceed to the Second Step – Perform Mathematical Calculations

In this discourse, you will undertake the task of determining the daily expenditure incurred by your tobacco dependency. Take a moment to acquire a calculator, a writing instrument, as well as some paper, and meticulously record your daily expenditures pertaining to cigarettes. Following this, proceed to calculate the corresponding estimates for a weekly, monthly, and annual basis. This encompasses expenditures pertaining to lighters and lighter fuel, matches, ashtrays, as well as materials such as papers and filters for smoking roll-ups. Please allocate a moment to deliberate upon the tangible acquisitions for yourself, your dear ones, your residence, or your automotive/ cycling assets that can be made possible by the funds saved upon cessation of smoking. Create a supplementary inventory of goods or possessions that have long been desired but remained financially unattainable until now, but will soon become accessible. This could encompass modest items such as a recently published book, or substantial investments like a brand-new refrigerator or oven, significant home improvements, a vacation overseas, or even persistent dental care that you have been deferring for an extensive period. Rest assured, by abstaining from purchasing tobacco as an individual within the average range of smoking habit, you will gradually accumulate a substantial amount of money that would enable you to pursue even your most ambitious aspirations. Now that you have examined the financial implications of your habit, begin envisioning the act of squandering a 50 pence coin with each instance of smoking a cigarette.

What is the reason behind your desire to cease tobacco consumption?

If you have participated in a therapy session, coaching call, or attended an event, you are likely accustomed to being queried as to the rationale behind your actions. This is because every action is propelled by an underlying motivation.

You initiated the habit of smoking with a purpose. It is imperative that you possess a valid justification for discontinuing the habit of smoking.

Irrespective of the duration of one's smoking habit, the act of quitting is regarded as an exceedingly daunting and occasionally arduous undertaking for individuals who smoke. For, how does one consciously and entirely relinquish that sensation of euphoria? Just like that?

Allow me to recount a brief anecdote...

Several years ago, a comrade expressed his intent to abstain from smoking indefinitely. After a thorough interrogation, he elucidated the reasons behind his initiation into smoking as well as his desire to cease the habit.

Following the demise of his mother, he involuntarily envisioned a future wherein he would reside exclusively with his father and two younger siblings.

Consequently, he was ill-equipped for the arrival of a new maternal figure or an interloper capable of diverting his father's focus away from him and his siblings. The mere idea of replacing his cherished mother compelled him to distance himself from his residence, where he encountered a new social circle that acquainted him with the habit of smoking.

In a single term, his derailment can be attributed to the influence of his "FAMILY".

Curiously, the reason for his desire to quit smoking lies in his strong emphasis on "FAMILY". He expressed a nostalgic smile and uttered, 'I long to reunite with them, partake in their company, and demonstrate the depth of my affection towards them.' I am aware that they would not object to my continued smoking, however, I am apprehensive that if I persist in this behavior, they will lose me unexpectedly. Despite his barely audible words, I perceived a sense of remorse regarding the time squandered.

Life is in stages. Failure to exercise restraint and deliberate control over one's thoughts, actions, and behavior may result in the profound consequence of remorse. The aforementioned destiny applies to smoking in equal measure.

Ceasing the habit of smoking yields numerous health advantages, a few of which may be familiar to you, such as experiencing improved cardiac and pulmonary well-being. These benefits are entirely logical and hold weight on multiple levels. Nevertheless, it has come to my attention that certain individuals do not place importance on the health advantages associated with quitting, as their motivations are often rooted in sentimentality and occasionally altruism. Shocking, I know.

Now, the choice to abstain from smoking is entirely subjective and each individual who smokes possesses one or multiple justifications. Based on my engagements and personal observations, the following elucidate the factors influencing individuals to discontinue smoking. You may also find that it is applicable in your case.

It is essential to ensure the safety and well-being of others.

Have you observed that when you engage in smoking in close proximity to individuals who do not smoke, they tend to relocate themselves or experience bouts of coughing? If you have not observed, it is possible that you have exhibited a high level of caution with regards to your smoking locations, or your attention has not been focused on this matter. For the purposes of documentation, the aforementioned response characterizes the physical sensations experienced by the cardiovascular, physiological, and respiratory systems with every instance of tobacco consumption.

Regardless, this inhalation of the gases emitted from your respiratory system is commonly referred to as secondhand smoke. And numerous individuals who engage in smoking, such as yourself, truly despise the negative impact it has on others in terms of their health, rather than in terms of societal acceptance.

The passing of a renowned vocalist is connected to this situation. He succumbed to smoke inhalation, despite having never ignited a single cigarette in his lifetime. A single existence tragically extinguished due to the actions of another individual.

Secondhand smoke refers to the inhalation of the smoke emitted by a cigarette that is breathed in by those in close proximity to the individual who is smoking. This gives rise to potential health hazards such as cardiovascular, pulmonary, and respiratory conditions, as well as a predisposition to asthma.

Upon cessation, you no longer subject your acquaintances, relatives, neighbors, and beloved individuals to the chemicals emanating from your cigarette.

Strategies For Ceasing The Habit Of Smoking

There exist various methods by which individuals effectively address their smoking addiction. Frequently, individuals who aspire to quit smoking ultimately find themselves relapsing into the very behaviors they sought to distance themselves from, owing to an inherent compulsion to revert. Ceasing an addiction is not a task accomplished in a short span of time; it entails persevering and refraining from a mere cessation of effort. Individuals who have effectively overcome their addiction have corroborated that frequently, they relapsed back into the same addictive behavior. There exist various approaches to smoking cessation; however, I wish to advocate for four distinct methods. These methodologies have been demonstrated to possess distinctiveness, as they contribute significantly and have been empirically validated. Are you prepared to cease your detrimental behaviors and exchange them for habits that are highly empowering? That is splendid news! Demonstrating unwavering dedication towards achieving a goal can culminate in successfully overcoming your tobacco dependency. Nonetheless, conquering this challenge will not be a straightforward endeavor. Nevertheless, adopting the most effective approach to halt this behavior is a significant stride towards ensuring its successful cessation. There exist numerous methodologies that individuals employ when they seek to cease their smoking habit. Certain individuals exhibit a higher propensity for expeditiously overcoming their addiction compared to others. The optimal approach is the one you can adhere to effortlessly and without encountering significant challenges. Please take into account the subsequent approaches that have proven successful for certain individuals in regards to ceasing to smoke:

1. (Without any external assistance), a method known as quitting cold turkey

2. Nicotine Replacement Therapy, commonly referred to as NRT, has been widely acknowledged for its high efficacy in aiding individuals in their endeavours to cease tobacco use."

3. Cognitive Behavioral Therapy is commonly referred to as (CBT) in academic and clinical circles.

4. Medical checkup.

5. Treatment combination.

1. COLD TURKEY (WITHOUT EXTERNAL ASSISTANCE) Merely 90% of the general populace attempting smoking cessation accomplish it unaided by social support, familial aid, external interventions such as therapy, or pharmaceutical assistance. While it is true that a

significant number of smokers attempt to quit abruptly, commonly known as the cold turkey method, only a limited proportion of individuals achieve success using this approach. This can be attributed to the inherent challenges associated with resisting the allure of temptation, leading many individuals to ultimately relent and continue their smoking habit. Approximately 5% to 7% of the overall population of smokers possess the ability to independently cease their smoking habit in due course. Dopamine has exerted significant influence over the cognitive faculties, causing the dopamine pathways to adopt a submissive disposition under the powerful sway of dopamine. The original purpose of our dopamine pathways was to generate a desire for sustenance, hydration, reproduction, and social interaction. However, once our dopamine pathway is subjected to enslavement, our mental priorities undergo a transformation, leading us to firmly believe that the consumption of nicotine on a regular basis surpasses all other aspects of life in importance, including our relationships, familial bonds, nourishment, romantic pursuits, adverse weather conditions, as well as our health and overall existence. Viewing drug addiction as simply a run-of-the-mill undesirable behavior undermines the gravity of its effects, as it possesses the capacity to exert influence, alter behavior, and assert dominance over individuals. The complete cessation of nicotine use is crucial for successful resolution of nicotine dependency. A fundamental principle that has proven effective for former addicts is the steadfast commitment to abstain from nicotine on a daily basis. Additionally, individuals may explore online resources such as websites and blogs as a means to engage in meaningful discussions and exchange thoughts with fellow ex-users. Social media serves as an effective platform to connect with individuals who are in similar circumstances, enabling the exchange of ideas and collaborative thinking, even in absence of physical interaction.

You are more than capable of achieving success.

Nothing is Impossible

By retaining a fervent aspiration, maintaining a sense of discipline and commitment, and cultivating a suitable mindset, there is virtually no limit to what you can achieve. The fact that you are currently perusing this book indicates that you already possess the aforementioned burning desire. While embarking on your journey towards achieving a smoke-free lifestyle, it is imperative to maintain an optimistic mindset and eradicate negativity from your thoughts. This type of mindset is undeniably a definitive formula for experiencing unsuccessful outcomes. Expunge the term cannot from your vocabulary and assert your unwavering determination to accomplish whatever you set your mind upon. Have unwavering faith and conviction in your heart, intellect, and essence. Adopt a perspective that focuses on the positive aspects of every situation, rather than dwelling on the negative, and wholeheartedly embrace it. This approach will enable you to effectively overcome and conquer this habit. Even in moments of temporary setback, it is important to practice self-compassion and avoid unnecessary self-criticism. Keep trying!

We're all different. Discontinuing this habit does not adhere to a universally applicable methodology. Varying approaches yield varying outcomes for individuals. Certain individuals may successfully cease smoking by abruptly discontinuing the habit, commonly referred to as going "cold turkey," whereas for others, a methodological approach may be necessary. Simply ascertain which approach suits you most effectively. I would be pleased to elucidate the measures I undertook to overcome smoking and offer valuable suggestions and strategies for your definitive cessation.

Similar to each of you, I myself encountered challenges in the process of quitting, which proved to be quite arduous. Nevertheless, I persevered by repeatedly making earnest attempts to cease the particular behavior. I persevered relentlessly, which ultimately led to my success.

This is the successful approach that I adopted

1- I have commenced the practice of consuming a volume of one gallon of water on a daily basis. Upon initiating the practice of consuming copious amounts of water, I observed a notable alteration in the taste of cigarettes, consequently diminishing my inclination to derive satisfaction from their consumption. Additionally, it served to reduce my urges.

Given my awareness that the craving would be temporary, I made necessary arrangements. During that time, I discovered various activities to engage in, such as reaching out to a friend, immersing myself in a book, strolling outdoors, engaging in jogging, or composing a blog.

3- Following each meal, I indulged in a lollipop as a means to quell my urges. Indeed, on every occasion that I experienced an inclination, I would indulge myself in the consumption of a lollipop. My spouse took the extra step to ensure that they were also devoid of any added sugars!

Engaging in physical activity turned into a recurring part of my daily routine. If you opt to incorporate a fitness regimen into your daily routine, it is advisable to commence gradually. I must acknowledge that I experienced breathlessness on numerous occasions. Indeed, on certain occasions, I entertained the belief that I was experiencing an episode of respiratory distress akin to an asthma attack.

Pay attention to the signals your body is giving you and refrain from exceeding your personal limitations. An initial time commitment of 30 minutes per day would be sufficient. In a matter of days, a significant transformation will become evident in your life. Your body's reliance will diminish, in turn providing you with an increased amount of vitality.

5-Practice deep breathing exercises. Utilizing proper breathing exercises will aid in breaking the habit, alleviating nicotine cravings, and enhancing pulmonary function.

Kindly inform your family, friends, and colleagues of your resolution to cease smoking. In particular, it is essential to prioritize maintaining relationships with your companions who smoke. Preserve the bonds of friendship, ensuring that they do not experience any sense of discomfort upon observing you passing by the designated smoking area during work hours. You would benefit from joining a support group. We all require supporters who can uplift us on our journey towards achieving our desired goals in life.

7- It would be advisable to consider making some modifications to your dietary regimen. I do not recommend any radical measures. Rather than removing the consumption of unhealthy foods, incorporate nutritive options. It is imperative to ensure an adequate intake of nutrients. If you consume carbonated beverages and indulge in an excessive amount of unhealthy snacks, endeavor to gradually reduce your intake. It is advisable to refrain from consuming junk foods and sugar as they have a tendency to exacerbate cravings. Just take it slow. It is not desirable to simultaneously experience cravings for cigarettes and a decline in blood sugar levels. Ensure that your dietary intake incorporates a significant amount of plant-based proteins. Incorporate sources of whole grains, seafood, legumes, dark leafy vegetables, carrot juice, celery, green salads, ample servings of carrots, as well as numerous citrus fruits to promote body alkalinity.

It is advised to refrain from consuming chocolate, cooked spinach, and rutabaga as they are foods that contribute to the formation of oxalic acid, leading to the binding of magnesium within the body.

One effective method of mitigating the presence of carcinogens in the body involves the consumption of a daily serving of green tea.

Utilize Chlorella as an efficient means to effectively rid your body of toxins.

Lobelia tea has been found to elicit a deterrence towards nicotine consumption and assist in managing cravings. To eliminate the presence of nicotine from your respiratory and immune systems, it is recommended to consume Echinacea or Ephedra tea.

Steer clear of any stimuli that incite your inclination to engage in smoking. Triggers pose a significant challenge for smokers, as they have the potential to precipitate relapse if not effectively managed and mitigated. In order to circumvent this issue, socialize with individuals who do not engage in smoking, frequent locations predominantly patronized by non-smokers, maintain a nutritious diet, and ensure an ample amount of rest.

9- The utmost crucial aspect of this entire procedure is to sustain a favorable disposition with an exceptionally constructive mindset. Approach each day individually and remain mindful of the motives underlying your decision to cease. Please refrain from being overly critical of yourself. In the event of an error, that is acceptable. Try again. Even though this procedure may present a level of difficulty, it is undoubtedly within the realm of feasibility.

It is possible that your initial day might not unfold flawlessly. One may likely encounter fluctuations in mood and perhaps even develop a strong aversion towards those in their vicinity, however, it is entirely conventional to experience such sentiments. In instances where you experience irritability, it would be beneficial to engage in physical activity such as taking a walk or, alternatively, engaging in a jog. Please remember to generously acknowledge your achievement of abstaining from smoking during the initial 24 hours by treating yourself accordingly.

I composed this book with the intention of reaching out to individuals who are grappling with nicotine addiction and are fatigued by its relentless hold, yet lack the knowledge or guidance to effectively initiate the process of quitting. I have a profound longing to provide empowerment for every reader through the dissemination of my personal narrative. Who could be more qualified than an individual who has successfully quit smoking to offer guidance on this subject? There was a time when I harbored uncertainty regarding my ability to discontinue, yet I eventually accomplished it. I never gave up. If there is nothing else you take away, I implore you to refrain from relinquishing your endeavors. It is your responsibility, both to yourself and to your loved ones.

3 – The Arrival of the Quit Date

At long last, the anticipated date has arrived. What steps should be taken in order to cease smoking in a manner that promotes good health? Outlined below are the crucial steps that need to be undertaken in order to permanently eradicate the lethal habit from one's life.

*) On the day you decide to quit smoking, adhere to the fundamental expectation of refraining from engaging in smoking. If feasible, it is recommended that you consider abstaining from smoking for a minimum of twelve hours prior to your planned cessation date. This will guarantee that you shall experience a rejuvenating start to your day. You will no longer experience the unpleasant breath caused by smoking, and it is worth noting that you are already ahead in adopting this life-saving habit.

*) Sustain a consistently active way of life. Make an effort to consistently visit the gym. Engage in a variety of physical pursuits at your residence or in open-air environments. If you possess a bicycle, it would be advisable to venture out into your residential vicinity rather than idling indoors. If you possess a canine companion, it is advisable to take him on a leisurely stroll across your locality.

*) Replenish your hydration levels frequently by consuming juices and ample quantities of water. Whenever one experiences an urge to smoke, it is advisable to hydrate oneself by drinking water. This will aid in the natural cleansing of nicotine from your bloodstream.

Furthermore, despite nicotine replacement therapy being presented as an option by healthcare professionals, it is advisable to opt for natural alternatives. You can overcome the addiction without administering any medication. Opting for complete naturalness is consistently the more advantageous decision from a standpoint of well-being.

Continuing to adhere to your established routine of participating in support group sessions and enrolling in smoking cessation courses would be advisable. Subsequently, augment those with strategic blueprints and self-improvement manuals. Additionally, computer software for smoking cessation can be downloaded, along with access to various supplementary resources pertaining to quitting smoking. Additionally, should you have a designated cessation hotline of your choice, please do not hesitate to utilize it at your discretion. This may be particularly beneficial in circumstances where you experience cravings or encounter exceptionally potent stimuli that prove challenging to cope with.

Ensure to steer clear from circumstances or stimuli that could potentially precipitate an adverse outcome. Please frequent establishments that enforce a smoke-free environment. Furthermore, it is advisable to occupy areas designated for non-smoking in establishments such as buildings, offices, malls, and airports.

Ensure that the acronym HALT is considered on a daily basis. The acronym HALT represents the avoidance of excessive hunger, anger, loneliness, and fatigue. These four stimuli can be consciously avoided as potent instigators.

Minimize the consumption of caffeine and alcohol, to the greatest extent possible. The consumption of alcohol can readily impair your cognitive faculties and hinder your ability to make rational decisions. It may serve as a convenient rationale for you to procure a cigarette. Moreover, there exists a demonstrable correlation between alcohol consumption and smoking. Conversely, caffeine often serves as a reminder of one's propensity for cigarettes. It is advisable to refrain from engaging in it in order to preempt any potential regrets.

Lastly, it is essential to acquaint yourself with the four A's of smoking as well. The initial A represents the concept of "Avoid." When confronted with individuals who may entice you to engage in smoking or environments that evoke memories of smoking, it is advisable to temporarily steer clear of them. When you believe you possess sufficient determination to resist the temptation, you may proceed to pay them another visit. The subsequent letter A represents the concept of "Alter." Consequently, it is advisable to modify your customary habits. If one has a predilection for alcohol and coffee, it would be advisable to consider consuming water or soda as alternatives.

When proceeding to your place of work, opt to traverse an alternate route. In lieu of engaging in a smoking break, consider taking a stroll. The subsequent letter symbolizes "Alternatives." Consider viable replacements capable of substituting cigarettes. Possible alternative: "It may comprise chewing gum, sunflower seeds, or even hard confections." Lastly, the final component denoted by the letter A signifies "Activities." To effectively occupy oneself to the extent of disregarding smoking as a habitual part of one's routine, it is imperative to engage in a diverse range of activities. They will prohibit or prevent you from engaging in smoking.

THE FUNCTIONALITY OF THE APPROACH

There will inevitably be uncertainties when implementing an untested methodology, leading to the emergence of critics seemingly out of nowhere.

The book entitled "EFFECTIVE STRATEGIES FOR LONG-TERM SMOKING CESSATION" provides valuable insights on the persuasion techniques to help individuals quit smoking permanently. Furthermore, I will elucidate my two-decade-long tenure as a tobacco user, expounding upon the successful measures I undertook to break free from this habit. At this point, you may understandably question the applicability of these strategies to your own circumstance. Rest assured, the efficacy of these approaches is substantiated by virtue of their origin in my own extensive experience as a smoker for the span of twenty years. I have indeed made efforts, encountered multiple failures, but also achieved success! I am confident that you will also experience similar outcomes.

This literature will not serve to enlighten you on the perils and risks associated with smoking, as it is a widely recognized matter. It will elucidate the process of embracing a smoke-free lifestyle, conveying the inherent joy and fulfillment of living devoid of the habit of smoking cigarettes. It is well-established knowledge that the data and statistics regarding the annual occurrences of deaths caused by smoking, as well as the detrimental effects that this profound addiction has on our health, are widely recognized. From a practical standpoint, smoking is widely recognized as one of the most arduous habits to break. It is a well-established fact that many individuals are cognizant of this challenge. Nonetheless, this literary work provides a straightforward solution for any smoker to successfully quit their addiction. You have indeed understood correctly; devoid of any ulterior motives or deceptive strategies, this uncomplicated piece of literature offers a straightforward account and educational content to facilitate a permanent cessation of smoking.

Stopping Gradually

Making a brief visit through the process of gradual disengagement. If you happen to be acquainted with an individual who strongly dislikes a smoker, it is advisable for you to actively promote the adoption of a reduction strategy, commonly known as gradual detachment. Contact them daily and instruct them to abstain from one cigarette.

In essence, if they typically engage in a daily habit of smoking forty cigarettes, they should strive to only smoke thirty-nine on the initial day of their cessation endeavor. Subsequently, on the succeeding day, they ought to limit their smoking to a mere thirty-eight, reducing it further to thirty-seven on the subsequent day, and continuing this pattern henceforth.

Subsequently, it would be beneficial to engage in daily communication with these individuals, extending congratulations and offering encouragement to sustain their efforts. I must reinforce my point by stating that this action should solely be carried out towards a smoker whom you truly abhor.

Gradually

The majority of individuals who smoke will concur with this proposed strategy. It appears to be quite straightforward to gradually reduce the number of cigarettes smoked each day. To a habitual smoker consuming two packs daily, a total of 39 cigarettes may appear inconsequential. The key lies in persuading the individual that your intentions are solely focused on assisting them.

During the initial week or two, the sole drawback is the necessity to feign affection towards the person and engage in daily conversations with them. They will also not complain excessively.

Once they have decreased their number from forty to thirty, they may occasionally express their dissatisfaction. You will not truly experience enjoyment at this point. The moment when the payoff materializes typically occurs approximately three weeks into the fraudulent endeavor. You have successfully reduced their quantity to less than half of their regular amount.

They experience consistent moderate withdrawal on a daily basis.

After one month of implementing the strategy, you have successfully induced significant withdrawal symptoms in them. But be relentless. Please contact them via telephone and express your admiration for their exceptional performance and convey your immense pride in their achievements. If the time frame falls within the thirty-fifth to thirty-ninth day, you have achieved a significant triumph.

This impoverished individual is experiencing severe isolation, enduring immense distress, and achieving no tangible outcomes as a result. They have made no progress in halting withdrawal since the commencement of the procedure. They are experiencing chronic withdrawal, refraining from indulging in just one or two per day, and instead subjecting themselves to a significant deprivation of thirty-five to forty daily.

If you intend to seize victory when your opponents have reached a score of zero, kindly inform them that in case circumstances become challenging, they need not be concerned but can instead find solace in occasionally indulging in a puff. If you are successful in eliciting their acceptance of this, and they subsequently adhere to a regimen of smoking only once every third day, they will perpetually experience symptoms of withdrawal.

Have I previously alluded to the fact that it is highly advisable to harbor a profound sense of disdain for this individual in order to engage in such actions towards them? It is plausible that this is the most malicious practical prank one may ever play on another individual. You will diminish their opportunity to cease smoking, subjecting them to prolonged suffering that may result in eventual resignation, returning to the habit with the same apprehension towards quitting that they experienced while reducing consumption, ultimately leading to continued smoking until it proves fatal. As previously mentioned, it would be advisable for you to harbor genuine disdain towards this individual.

With any luck, you do not harbor such intense animosity towards anyone to enact such a course of action upon them. I have confidence that no one possesses such a low self-regard as to inflict such harm upon themselves. Ceasing abruptly might prove challenging, yet discontinuing via this withdrawal method is scarcely achievable.

If faced with a choice between difficult and unfeasible, opting for the former is advisable. Upon completion of a arduous endeavor, you shall possess tangible evidence of your accomplishment, whereas embarking upon an impractical approach shall yield naught but misery.

Cease abruptly and after a period of seventy-two hours, the symptoms gradually diminish. Reducing the current level of activity is likely to result in a gradual deterioration over an extended period, spanning weeks, months, or even years, if left unaddressed.

Strategies for Breaking the Smoking Habit

Given all the aforementioned factors, as well as numerous others, I would appreciate the opportunity to discuss the necessary steps to overcome the habit of smoking.

One challenge encountered while attempting to cease smoking is the lingering sensation of emptiness we experience. We perceive a void in our existence. As the frequency of smoking increases, so does the number of triggers that activate the craving for smoking, consequently making it increasingly challenging to quit.

Our cognitive faculties are inclined towards perseverance rather than abandonment of activities, while exhibiting significant aptitude for assimilating new habits. In this book, I aim to discuss an alternative approach whereby rather than solely attempting to cease smoking, our focus will be on substituting your unfavorablebehaviors with more positive ones. In adopting this approach, you can perpetually evade the experience of inner void. One does not encounter the repercussions of gaining an additional ten pounds when attempting to abstain, merely substituting one health issue with another. On the contrary, as your self-perception improves, your general state of being will correspondingly ameliorate.

We intend to leverage your body's remarkable capacity for habit formation to combat the inclination to smoke in an unprecedented manner. The sector of your cognitive faculty responsible for relinquishing habits exhibits limited strength and is susceptible to diversionary influences, whereas the sector involved in habit formation showcases remarkable fortitude due to its role in enhancing bodily efficiency. It consolidates a collection of tasks into a unified task, records said process, and stores it within your long-term memory.

That is the strategic location where we anticipate achieving victory in our campaign against tobacco consumption. We will commence by modifying something of utmost importance. The primary cause of the majority's inability to successfully discontinue a habit, including your own previous unsuccessful attempts, can be attributed to a straightforward factor. You were attempting to discontinue engaging in an activity that you desired to pursue.

On every occasion when I attempted to cease smoking in the previous instances, I was confronted with an internal conflict, as a portion of my being was inclined towards perpetuating the habit. Although 80 percent of my being desired to cease, the remaining 20 percent yearned for the sensation, the resonance, the ceremonial act, that initial intake of nicotine to enter the bloodstream. That is precisely the factor that impedes our progress.

Allow me to impart upon you the method of substituting your inclination towards smoking with a sensation of repugnance. Currently, smoking is an abhorrent and repulsive behavior in my opinion. Upon witnessing individuals engage in smoking, I find it visually unappealing. I do not gaze upon that cigarette with yearning, and as a result, I have found it remarkably effortless to resist any inclination to revert to being a smoker.

Post-resignation Life Expectations" "Perspectives on Life Following Resignation" "Prospects in the Wake of Your Departure" "The Outlook for Your Future Beyond Quitting

One of the most exquisite aspects of quitting smoking is that one's life undergoes an immediate transformation. Upon the lapse of fifteen minutes, you shall commence to observe the initial improvements in your health.

It is a gradual process that may require some time investment, but you will gradually observe an enhancement in your physical strength, speed, and overall bodily proficiency. Respiration becomes slightly more effortless. Regrettably, the path to achieving a state of optimal health is a protracted one. It may require a period of up to fifteen years for complete restoration from the duration of smoking. Hence, it is of utmost importance that we commence without delay, while keeping in mind that you have support along the way.

A survey conducted by the Centers for Disease Control and Prevention in 2015 revealed that a significant majority of smokers, accounting for 68 percent, expressed their inclination and desire to cease tobacco consumption. This implies that in a gathering of ten individuals where smoking is taking place, a substantial majority of seventy percent divulge their desire to discontinue this habit. This constitutes the prevailing view, despite the fact that our silence may lead us to believe that everyone desires to continue smoking.

Imagine "Future You"

I kindly request you to take a brief moment and envisage the potentiality of your future.

How would one's experience change if they were to abstain from smoking? What is the experience of relinquishing control over one's emotions and behaviors? What is the experience of being liberated from a habit that is despised? What is the sensation of experiencing the elongation of one's life? Now, rather than expressing concern about experiencing a decline in health during one's fifties or sixties, the focus has shifted to contemplating the possibility of extending one's lifespan to the remarkable ages of one hundred or even one hundred and twenty.

The funds previously allocated towards cigarettes and associated taxes can now be redirected towards fostering constructive interests and pastimes, such as purchasing cinema tickets or contributing to your children's college education. Upon examining the figures, it is evident that the annual expenditure on smoking can be quite staggering.

Envision the prospect of waking up each morning without experiencing the discomfort of coughing, devoid of the compulsion to ignite a cigarette, and liberated from the concern of preserving the resale value of your vehicle by refraining from smoking within it. Abruptly, you arise and a more radiant day ensues. You are not experiencing any shortness of breath. As you descend the staircase, a surge of strength and vitality engulfs you, filling you with eagerness to wholeheartedly embrace the experiences that lie ahead. One experiences a profound liberation that has been absent for an extended period of time.

www.ingramcontent.com/pod-product-compliance
Lightning Source LLC
Chambersburg PA
CBHW052140110526
44591CB00012B/1798